Wright

D1149642

by Iain Gray

Lang**Syne**

PUBLISHING

WRITING *to* REMEMBER

Lang**Syne**

PUBLISHING

WRITING *to* REMEMBER

79 Main Street, Newtongrange,
Midlothian EH22 4NA
Tel: 0131 344 0414   Fax: 0845 075 6085
E-mail: info@lang-syne.co.uk
www.langsyneshop.co.uk

Design by Dorothy Meikle
Printed by Fixture Displays, China
© Lang Syne Publishers Ltd 2013

ISBN 978-1-85217-380-7

Wright

NAME variations include:
Right
Write
Wrighte

The spirit of the clan means
much to thousands of people

Chapter one:

The origins of the clan system

by Rennie McOwan

The original Scottish clans of the Highlands and the great families of the Lowlands and Borders were gatherings of families, relatives, allies and neighbours for mutual protection against rivals or invaders.

Scotland experienced invasion from the Vikings, the Romans and English armies from the south. The Norman invasion of what is now England also had an influence on land-holding in Scotland. Some of these invaders stayed on and in time became 'Scottish'.

The word clan derives from the Gaelic language term 'clann', meaning children, and it was first used many centuries ago as communities were formed around tribal lands in glens and mountain fastnesses.

The format of clans changed over the centuries, but at its best the chief and his family held the land on behalf of all, like trustees, and the ordinary clansmen and women believed they had a blood relationship with the founder of their clan.

There were two way duties and obligations. An inadequate chief could be deposed and replaced by someone of greater ability.

Clan people had an immense pride in race. Their relationship with the chief was like adult children to a father and they had a real dignity.

The concept of clanship is very old and a more feudal notion of authority gradually crept in.

Pictland, for instance, was divided into seven principalities ruled by feudal leaders who were the strongest and most charismatic leaders of their particular groups.

By the sixth century the 'British' kingdoms of Strathclyde, Lothian and Celtic Dalriada (Argyll) had emerged and Scotland, as one nation, began to take shape in the time of King Kenneth MacAlpin.

Some chiefs claimed descent from ancient kings which may not have been accurate in every case.

By the twelfth and thirteenth centuries the clans and families were more strongly brought under the central control of Scottish monarchs.

Lands were awarded and administered more and more under royal favour, yet the power of the area clan chiefs was still very great.

The long wars to ensure Scotland's

independence against the expansionist ideas of English monarchs extended the influence of some clans and reduced the lands of others.

Those who supported Scotland's greatest king, Robert the Bruce, were awarded the territories of the families who had opposed his claim to the Scottish throne.

In the Scottish Borders country – the notorious Debatable Lands – the great families built up a ferocious reputation for providing warlike men accustomed to raiding into England and occasionally fighting one another.

Chiefs had the power to dispense justice and to confiscate lands and clan warfare produced a society where martial virtues – courage, hardiness, tenacity – were greatly admired.

Gradually the relationship between the clans and the Crown became strained as Scottish monarchs became more orientated to life in the Lowlands and, on occasion, towards England.

The Highland clans spoke a different language, Gaelic, whereas the language of Lowland Scotland and the court was Scots and in more modern times, English.

Highlanders dressed differently, had different

customs, and their wild mountain land sometimes seemed almost foreign to people living in the Lowlands.

It must be emphasised that Gaelic culture was very rich and story-telling, poetry, piping, the clarsach (harp) and other music all flourished and were greatly respected.

Highland culture was different from other parts of Scotland but it was not inferior or less sophisticated.

Central Government, whether in London or Edinburgh, sometimes saw the Gaelic clans as a challenge to their authority and some sent expeditions into the Highlands and west to crush the power of the Lords of the Isles.

Nevertheless, when the eighteenth century Jacobite Risings came along the cause of the Stuarts was mainly supported by Highland clans.

The word Jacobite comes from the Latin for James – Jacobus. The Jacobites wanted to restore the exiled Stuarts to the throne of Britain.

The monarchies of Scotland and England became one in 1603 when King James VI of Scotland (1st of England) gained the English throne after Queen Elizabeth died.

The Union of Parliaments of Scotland and England, the Treaty of Union, took place in 1707.

Some Highland clans, of course, and Lowland families opposed the Jacobites and supported the incoming Hanoverians.

After the Jacobite cause finally went down at Culloden in 1746 a kind of ethnic cleansing took place. The power of the chiefs was curtailed. Tartan and the pipes were banned in law.

Many emigrated, some because they wanted to, some because they were evicted by force. In addition, many Highlanders left for the cities of the south to seek work.

Many of the clan lands became home to sheep and deer shooting estates.

But the warlike traditions of the clans and the great Lowland and Border families lived on, with their descendants fighting bravely for freedom in two world wars.

Remember the men from whence you came, says the Gaelic proverb, and to that could be added the role of many heroic women.

The spirit of the clan, of having roots, whether Highland or Lowland, means much to thousands of people.

*Clan warfare produced a society where courage
and tenacity were greatly admired*

Chapter two:

Workers and warriors

Derived from the Old English 'wrytha', or 'wyrhtha', indicating 'work', Wright is a name that denotes someone who makes things, or 'wroughts' – for example a wheelwright who makes wheels or a shipwright who makes ships.

In Scotland, however, in a number of confusing early variations of spelling such as 'Wrycht', the name was more specifically held to denote a carpenter or joiner, or someone who worked with wood in general.

The name makes its appearance in the Scottish historical records in the late thirteenth century, particularly through what is known as the infamous Ragman Roll of 1296 – an invaluable document with regard to early surnames.

It was in July of that year that the Scots rose in revolt against the imperialist designs of England's Edward I, but, living up to his reputation of 'Hammer of the Scots', he brought the entire nation under his subjugation little less than a month later.

To reinforce his domination, 1,500 earls,

bishops and burgesses were required to sign a humiliating treaty of fealty, known as the Ragman Roll, because of the number of ribbons that dangled from the seals of the reluctant signatories.

Among these are a William Wrycht and a Thomas Wrycht, both from Lanarkshire, and a Rauf le Wrighte of Stirling – indicating that these bearers of the name had achieved a fair degree of social standing and wealth.

The surname is also recorded from about this period in Berwickshire, in the Scottish Borders, while many of the name to be found today in Northern Ireland may well be descendants of Wrights who settled there in the early years of the seventeenth century.

This was through the policy known as 'plantation' under which Scottish Protestants received land grants in Ulster at the expense of what were perceived as rebellious native Irish clans.

Wrights of today can also claim a special bond of kinship with the Scottish clan of Macintyre, or MacIntyre.

The reasons for this stretch back through the dim mists of time to the age of the colourful twelfth century King of the Isles, Somerled, or Somhairle, whose name means 'summer voyager', and who was killed in battle near Renfrew on the west coast of the Scottish mainland in 1164.

Somerled, according to legend, had for some time sought the hand in marriage of the beautiful Ragnhilda, daughter of the Norse King of Man Olav the Red.

The Norse king, for dynastic reasons, was not keen on the match, but the cunning Somerled prepared a plan to further his aim.

Agreeing to join Olav on a sea raid on the island of Skye, he arranged before the attack for a shipwright, known as Maurice Mac Niall, to secretly bore holes in the hull of Olav's ship then fill them with tallow to provide a temporary seal.

On the night of the planned raid, as Olav's vessel surged through the sea en route to Skye, it began to take on water.

In imminent danger of sinking, he called on Somerled to come to his aid – but he steadfastly refused until the Norse king consented to the marriage.

Somerled then instructed the faithful Maurice to fill the holes with wooden plugs that he had crafted earlier.

Maurice is said to have been rewarded by Somerled with the grant of the lands of Glen Noe, near Oban on the west coast of Scotland, and his descendants became known in Gaelic as 'Mac-an-t-soir', 'sons of the carpenter', or 'sons of the wright' – later 'Macintyre'.

This is why the Wrights of today, along with others that include the Tyres and MacTears, are considered a sept, or sub-branch of the Macintyres – whose motto is 'Through difficulties' or 'The safest hope is in heaven' and whose crest is a hand holding a dirk, or dagger.

As a sept of Clan Macintyre, the Wrights shared in both its glorious fortunes and tragic misfortunes – most notable of the latter being the ill-fated Jacobite Rising of 1745 when, in April of the following year, a branch of the clan known as the Macintyres of Badenoch were among the many slain by the Hanoverians at the battle of Culloden.

Bearers of the Wright name have gained distinction in much later conflicts, with no less than three being awarded the Victoria Cross (VC), the highest award for bravery in the face of enemy action for British and Commonwealth forces.

Born in 1826 in Ballymena, Co. Antrim, Alexander Wright was an Irish recipient of the honour.

It was as a private in the 77th (East

Middlesex) Regiment of Foot during the Crimean War that, in March of 1855 at the siege of Sebastopol, he single-handedly repelled an enemy attack, while three weeks later he was instrumental, despite his wounds, in capturing an enemy trench.

He survived the war and died in 1858.

It was during a British military campaign in Nigeria known as the Kano-Sokoto Expedition, that Brigadier General Wallace Wright, then a 28-year-old lieutenant in the 1st Battalion, The Queen's Royal West Surrey Regiment, won his VC.

This was in February of 1903 when, with only 44 men, he held off an enemy charge.

Later promoted to Brigadier General, he died in 1953.

Born in Brighton in 1883, Theodore Wright was a posthumous recipient of the VC during the First World War.

He had been a captain in the 57th Field Company, Corps of Royal Engineers when, in August of 1914 at Mons, in Belgium, he and a fellow officer braved heavy fire to connect up the electric leads to a demolition charge placed on a bridge.

He was killed only a few days later while helping a wounded man into shelter.

His medal is displayed at the Royal Engineers Museum, in Kent.

Across the Atlantic, Admiral Jerauld Wright was the highly decorated American naval officer who was born in 1898 in Amherst, Massachusetts.

Serving in both the European and Pacific theatres during the Second World War and recognised as an expert in naval gunnery, he later served, from 1954 to 1960, as Supreme Allied Commander (Atlantic) for NATO.

With nicknames that included "Old Iron Heels" and "El Supremo", he was also responsible during the Cold War for overseeing the reorganisation of the U.S. Navy's Atlantic fleet.

In retirement, he and the retired British Admiral Sir Nigel Henderson led the initiative for the restoration on the Arbigland estate, near Kirkbean, in Kirkcudbright, in the southwest of Scotland, of the cottage that was the eighteenth century birthplace of John Paul Jones, the Scot recognised as "Father of the American Navy."

Now fully restored and housing a museum, the cottage opened to the public two years before Admiral Wright's death in 1995.

In a conflict with a particular resonance at the

time of writing, Corporal Mark Wright, born in Edinburgh in 1979, was a posthumous recipient of the George Cross.

This was for his valour when, serving with the 3rd Battalion of the Parachute Regiment in Helmand Province, Afghanistan, he was killed in September of 2006 after entering a minefield to rescue injured comrades.

It was in his honour that Mark Wright House, a dedicated centre for army personnel recovering from their injuries, was opened in his native Edinburgh in August of 2009.

Chapter three:

Taking to the skies

Away from the battlefield, Wrights have also gained distinction in a range of more peaceful pursuits.

Two of the most famous bearers of the name were the brothers Wilbur and Orville Wright, the pioneering American aviators who made the world's first controlled, powered and heavier-than-air human flight.

Wilbur, born in 1867 in Millville, Ohio, and Orville, born four years later in Dayton, Ohio, are said to have had their fascination with flying first aroused when, as young lads, their father gave them a present of a toy 'helicopter' based on a design by the French aeronautical pioneer Alphonse Rénaud.

Gifted with extraordinary mechanical skills, the brothers set up in business manufacturing and repairing everything from bicycles and motors to printing presses, and this was to stand them in good stead when they came to build their first flying machines.

This culminated on December 17, 1903, at Kitty Hawk, North Carolina, when an aircraft made from machinery and other materials cobbled together in their workshop, took to the air.

In separate flights, one of twelve seconds duration, one of 59 seconds and at an altitude of approximately 10ft, they flew lengths of 120ft and 852 ft respectively.

The rudimentary machine was later perfected as the Wright Flyer I, and the brothers went on to invent aircraft controls that made fixed wing flight possible.

Wilbur died only nine years after the historic flights, while his brother died in 1948, by which time aviation had truly come of age.

Their original aeroplane, made of spruce and powered by a petrol engine, is now on display in the Smithsonian in Washington, along with a plaque that records how:

'By original scientific research the Wright brothers discovered the principles of human flight. As inventors, builders and flyers they further developed the aeroplane, taught man to fly and opened the era of aviation.'

Still looking to the skies and much further beyond, William Wright, born in 1871 in San Francisco, was the American astronomer who, as director from 1935 to 1942 of the Lick Observatory, became famous for his work on the velocity of stars in our galaxy. A recipient of the 1938 Gold Medal of the Royal Astronomical Society, he died in 1959, while the moon crater 'Wright' is named in his honour.

One bearer of the Wright name whose legacy survives as part of the urban landscape of America is Frank Lloyd Wright, who was born in 1867 in Richland Center, Wisconsin.

A promoter of the 'organic' school of architecture, Wright, who died in 1959, has been recognised by the American Institute of Architects as 'the greatest American architect of all time.'

Architect of more than 500 structures that include his own summer home of Taliesin near Spring Green, Wisconsin, the house known as Fallingwater in the mountains of Penna on Bear Run Creek, New York's Guggenheim Museum, his 1904 Unity Temple in Oak Park, Illinois and the Frank Lloyd Wright Home and Studio, also in Oak Park, Wright was honoured on a U.S. postage stamp issued in 1966.

From urban America to the far flung and frozen reaches of Antarctica, Sir Charles Seymour Wright, also known as Silas Wright, born in 1887 in Toronto, was one of the intrepid members of Captain Robert Scott's ill-fated Terra Nova expedition of 1910 to 1913.

The young Canadian physicist and glaciologist was a member of the original team that set off with Scott from base camp at Cape Evans with the aim of reaching the South Pole.

Wright was among a supporting party that Scott sent back to base. Several months later he was the first to spot the tent containing the frozen bodies of Scott, Henry Bowers and Edmund Wilson.

Enlisting with the British Army's Royal Engineers during the First World War, he developed the trench wireless, while during the Second World War he developed devices to detect magnetic mines.

Knighted in 1946 for his war service, he died in 1975.

One particularly enterprising bearer of the Wright name was William Henry Wright who, starting off his working life as a butcher's apprentice, ended as an immensely wealthy gold mine owner and the founder of what flourishes today as Canada's national newspaper.

Better known as Bill Wright, and born in 1876 in Sleaford, Lincolnshire he swapped the apron of a butcher's apprentice for British Army uniform in 1897, serving throughout the Boer War in South Africa.

Immigrating to Canada in 1907, he joined his

sister and her husband Edward Hargreaves, who had settled in northern Ontario.

Wright worked for a time with his brother-in-law, a master butcher, before the pair decided to seek their fortune by prospecting for gold.

It was in the Kirkland Lake region of northern Ontario that, one memorable evening in July of 1911, Hargreaves became lost while hunting for rabbits for their evening meal.

He fired a rifle shot to attract his brother-in-law's attention, and it was while Wright was walking towards the sound that he stopped in his tracks after blundering into an outcrop of quartz.

Even in the fading light, he was able to spot flecks of gold.

Confirming this when he and Hargreaves returned to the spot in the better light of the following morning, they subsequently staked a number of claims on the land over the following weeks.

But the claims had to be more carefully examined, and the partnership between the pair ended for a time when Hargreaves decided to return from the wilds of Kirkland Lake to support his wife.

Braving the harsh conditions on his own, Wright persisted in further exploration, and the area that he staked out eventually resulted in the three gold mines of Lakeshore, Sylvanite and Wright-Hargreaves – from which an astonishing 13.5 million ounces of gold were extracted over the years.

Despite the immense wealth the former butcher's apprentice and soldier had accrued only five years after his original discovery, and the fact that he was nearly 40 years of age, Wright insisted on enlisting as a private in the Canadian Army in 1916.

He served with distinction on the Western Front, turning down the opportunity of promotion several times.

Returning to his mining interests at the end of the First World War, he built up what became one of Canada's major mining companies.

In 1936, fifteen years before his death, he used part of his vast fortune to acquire the two Toronto newspapers *The Globe* and *The Mail and Empire* and, along with George McCullagh, merged them as *The Globe and Mail* – Canada's leading national newspaper of today.

Chapter four:

On the world stage

Proud bearers of the Wright name have also excelled in other pursuits that include entertainment, sport and the arts.

Best known for her role as Ginny Weasley in the *Harry Potter* series of films, **Bonnie Wright** is the English actress who was born in London in 1991.

It was after her brother, an avid fan of J.K. Rowling's series of *Harry Potter* books, told her that she reminded him of the character, that she successfully auditioned for the first film in the series, the 2001 *Harry Potter and the Philosopher's Stone*.

She has since appeared in all the other film adaptations of the book, including the 2010 *Harry Potter and the Deathly Hallows: Part I*, while, at the time of writing, she is set to appear in *Deathly Hallows: Part II*, scheduled for release in 2011.

Although born in London, it was in the United States that **Ben Wright** made his name as an actor on radio, television and film.

Born in 1915, he later settled in America, where from 1949 to 1950 he was the voice of

Sherlock Holmes in a popular radio series of the name and, from 1951 to 1952, as Inspector Peter Black in the *Pursuit* series. Wright, who died in 1989, also appeared in films that include *The Sound of Music* and *My Fair Lady*, while he was also the narrator for the 1963 film *Cleopatra*.

Married to the American actor Rip Torn, **Amy Wright** is the actress born in Chicago in 1950 whose films include the 1995 *The Scarlet Letter*, while on television **Gillian Wright** is the British actress best known for her role as Jean Slater in the popular BBC soap *EastEnders*.

The actress, who was born Gillian Hambidge in 1959 in Carshalton, south London, was a recipient in 2006 of a Mental Health Media Award for her character portrayal in *EastEnders* of a bipolar disorder sufferer.

Behind the camera lens, **Herbert Wright**, born in 1947 in Columbas, Indiana and who died in 2005, was the science fiction writer and producer best known for his work on *Star Trek: The Next Generation*, while **Joe Wright** is the English film director, born in London in 1972, who won a 2003 BAFTA Award for Best Serial Drama for *Charles II: The Power and the Passion*.

Best known as the co-creator, along with

Jonathan Glassner, of the television series *Stargate SG-1*, **Brad Wright** is the Canadian television producer, screenwriter and actor who was born in Toronto in 1961, while in the heat of the kitchen **Clarissa Dickson Wright** is a British celebrity chef.

Born in 1947 in St John's Wood, London she is best known as having been one half, along with the late Jennifer Paterson, of the 1990's television food series *Two Fat Ladies*.

Bearers of the Wright name have also excelled, and continue to excel, in the highly competitive world of sport.

On the tennis court, **Beals Wright** was the leading American player from Boston who was U.S. Singles Champion in 1905 and Doubles Champion in 1904, 1905 and 1906.

The player, who was born in 1879, was inducted into the International Tennis Hall of Fame five years before his death in 1961.

From tennis to the fields of European football, **Billy Wright** was the talented English centre half who was the first footballer in the world to earn 100 caps playing for his country, captaining the England team on no less than 90 occasions between 1946 and 1959.

Born in 1924 in Ironbridge, Shropshire he

spent his entire playing career with Wolverhampton Wanderers – from 1939 to 1959 – while he was inducted into the English Football Hall of Fame in 2002, eight years after his death.

Now a radio and television personality, **Ian Wright** is the former English footballer who played for teams that include Crystal Palace, Arsenal, Celtic and Burnley.

The striker, born in London in 1963, earned 33 caps playing for his country between 1991 and 1998.

In American football, **Anthony Wright** is the retired quarterback, born in 1976 in Vanceboro, North Carolina, who played for teams that include the Pittsburgh Steelers and, from 2007 to 2008, the New York Giants.

His namesake, **Anthony Wright**, is the field hockey sweeper, born in 1984 in Vancouver, who was a member of the Canadian national team that took gold at the 2007 Pan American Games.

On the golf course, **Pamela Wright**, born in 1964, is the Scottish professional golfer who played on the ladies European Tour and was a member of the European Solheim Cup team in the early 1990s.

Bearers of the Wright name have also left

their mark on the landscape in the form of notable civil engineering projects.

Known as "the Father of American Civil Engineering", **Benjamin Wright** was the American engineer, born in 1770 in Wethersfield, Connecticut who served as chief engineer of both the Erie and the Chesapeake and Ohio canals in the early decades of the nineteenth century.

Another leading civil engineer was **Horatio Wright**, who also served as a general with the Union Army during the American Civil War of 1861 to 1865.

After the war Wright, who was born in 1820 in Clinton, Massachusetts and who died in 1899, was responsible for projects that included completion of the Washington Monument and New York's Brooklyn Bridge.

Fort Horatio Wright, on the eastern tip of New York's Fishers Island, is named in his honour.

In the creative world of art, **Andy Wright** is the Canadian multi-media artist, born in 1971, whose best known work is the stunning video installation *Blind Man's Buff* and who has been nominated several times for Canada's prestigious Sobey Art Award.

In a different artistic genre, **David Wright**, born in 1944 and who died in 1967, was the British illustrator best known for his creation in 1956 of the *Daily Mail* newspaper's *Carol Day* cartoon strip, and for his series of illustrations for *The Sketch*.

Born in 1917, **Doug Wright** was the English-born Canadian cartoonist who created the famous and long-running Canadian newspaper comic strip *Doug Wright's Family*.

The cartoonist, who died in 1983, is honoured through Canada's annual Doug Wright awards, established in 2005 to recognise Canadian cartoonists and graphic artists.

In the equally creative world of literature, Carolyn D. Wright, better known as **C.D. Wright**, is the contemporary American poet, born in 1949 in Mountain Home, Arkansas whose works include the 1986 *Further Adventures with You* and the 2009 *40 Watts*.

Born in 1985 in Pickwick Dam, Tennessee, **Charles Wright** is the American poet who won the 1998 Pulitzer Prize for Poetry for his *Black Zodiac*, while another Pulitzer Prize winner is **Doug Wright**, the American playwright and screenwriter, born in 1962 in Dallas, who won the 2004 Pulitzer Prize for Drama for his play *I Am My Own Wife*.

Winner of no less than three of Canada's

major literary awards – the Giller Prize, the Trillium Book Award and the Governor General's Award – **Richard B. Wright** is the Canadian novelist born in 1937 in Ontario.

It was for his 2001 novel *Callan* that he won the awards, while other honours of which he is a recipient are membership of the Order of Canada and an Honorary Doctor of Letters from Trent University.

Born in 1939 in Saskatoon, Saskatchewan, Laurali Rose Wright, better known as **L.R. Wright**, was the best-selling Canadian writer of mystery novels whose final novel, *Menace*, was published in 2001, the year of her death.

A fashion model and photographer in addition to children's author, **Dare Wright**, born in 1914 in Thornhill, Ontario and later moving with her family to Cleveland, Ohio, was the author of books that include *The Lonely Doll* and *Edith and the Duckling*; she died in 2001.

From the world of the written word to the world of music, **Betty Wright**, born in 1953 in Miami, Florida is the Grammy Award-winning rhythm and blues and soul singer recognised as having influenced the development of the hip-hop genre.

Her 1975 single *Where is the Love* won a

Grammy for best rhythm and blues song, while other hits include the 1989 *Keep Love New*.

Known as 'The Prince of the Blues', **Billy Wright**, born in 1932 in Atlanta and who died in 1991, was the American 'jump blues' artiste whose hits include the 1949 *Blues for My Baby* and the 1959 *Have Mercy, Baby*.

In contemporary music **Chely Wright**, born in Kansas City in 1970, is the country music singer who had a No. 1 American hit in 1999 with the single *White Female*.

Considered to have been one of the founders of the 'gangsta rap' genre, Eric Lynn Wright, born in 1963 in Compton, California and better known as **Eazy-E**, was the American rapper and record producer whose hit albums include the 1988 *Eazy-Duz-It*; he died in 1995.

Born in 1943 in Middlesex, **Richard Wright** was the songwriter, vocalist and keyboardist with the British progressive rock band Pink Floyd; he died in 2008.

Born in 1972 in Frankfurt, Germany, the son of an American helicopter pilot during the Vietnam War, Frank Edwin Wright III is the drummer for the American punk band Green Day better known by his rather more colourful stage name of **Tré Cool**.

One particularly controversial bearer of the Wight name was the British scientist and counter-intelligence officer **Peter Wright**.

Born in 1916 in Chesterfield, Derbyshire he served during the Second World War with the Admiralty Research Laboratory, and was later recruited as principal scientific officer for the British intelligence agency MI5.

It was shortly after his retirement from MI5 and subsequent move to Australia that, in 1985, his sensational and best-selling memoirs were published as *Spycatcher* – a book that the British authorities unsuccessfully fought through the courts to suppress on the grounds that it breached the Official Secrets Act.

The book made newspaper headlines around the world, with Wright's claims that not only had the agency he had worked for been involved in the illegal planting of listening devices, or 'bugs', but also that a secret group within MI5 had been involved in a plot in the 1970s to remove the then Labour Prime Minister Harold Wilson from power.

Wright, who also controversially claimed that the former Soviet intelligence agency the KGB had infiltrated a number of British institutions, including MI5 itself, died in 1995.